The Art of Growing Old

by Herbert Vander Lugt

CONTENTS

INTRODUCTION

During my late teens I asked a man crowding his seventies if he envied those of us who were young. He replied something like this: "No, Herbert, I don't. I'm glad to be just exactly where I am in life. I'm not afraid to die. I'm not tired of living. But neither would I like to go back and repeat all the trials and failures of my past." His cheerful ways had always impressed me favorably, and now this answer confirmed my good feeling toward him. I saw him as a man who was growing old with grace, dignity, and good humor.

A little more than four decades have slipped by since that day. I have seen scores of my loved ones and friends grow old and die. I have talked and prayed and wept with many of them in times of crisis. I have watched some of them as their spirits slipped away, and then I have turned to comfort their survivors.

In all of these experiences I have found that Christians who follow biblical principles, and who fellowship with the Lord, can face serenely the special difficulties and trials associated with the autumn years. And in this book I'm offering some practical guidelines for all who want to be joyous, delightful, and God-honoring senior citizens.

I pray that the Holy Spirit will make these biblical truths living realities for every reader.

Herbert Vander Lugt

1
THAT AWESOME REALIZATION

When people enter their late forties or early fifties, they start getting reminders that tell them they are more than half way through life's earthly journey. These implications of personal mortality come in different ways. Sometimes they accompany the death of a friend or loved one. Occasionally a person recollects something that happened 20 years ago, suddenly realizes how quickly time goes by, and finds himself thinking, "Wow! I'll be 70 before I know it." The awareness of life's brevity may come with a jolt when a person finds out he has high blood pressure or other physical problems that are usually associated with aging.

A clean-living, faithful believer who was beginning to show some symptoms of a serious heart malady said to me, "For the first time I find myself thinking about my own death, and I'm shook up. I've always known I could be killed in an accident or die from a disease like cancer, but I viewed *this* as a remote possibility. I had so much living to do that I didn't think much about dying. But now I find myself saying, 'Dear God, my body is breaking down. I know I'm going to die, and I don't like it.' "

I don't think this is an unusual experience, not even for sincere Christians. It is not necessarily an indication of low spirituality. This keen and new awareness of one's own temporary existence can come as a shock to anybody, and it must be dealt with like any other spiritual problem. The non-Christian who comes face-to-face with his mortality can do nothing better than view it with stoicism, but a child of God can deal with his fear of death in such a way that he will reach a higher spiritual plateau than he ever enjoyed before.

Learning to handle gracefully the awareness of one's vulnerability to death is a major facet in the art of growing old. Some of God's children do this very well, but others don't. I am convinced that the unsaved would pay much more attention to our testimony if they would see us facing the fact of our mortality with a calmness and confidence, which they admit they do not have.

As I see it, living triumphantly with the

realization that one is running the last laps of the earthly race includes these three elements: (1) an open and cheerful acknowledgment of reality, (2) a resolute trust in God, and (3) an awareness of life's purpose.

AN ACKNOWLEDGMENT OF REALITY

The first characteristic which ought to mark every Christian in his senior adult years is an open and cheerful acknowledgment of reality. If you are 50, you must face up to the fact that according to the law of averages you have gone about two-thirds of the way through your earthly journey. True, you may be that exceptional person who will live to be 100 years old, but then again you may be one of those who die in their fifties or sixties. Many people do.

I recall quite vividly the feeling I had as I stood at the bedside of Dr. M. R. De Haan shortly before the Lord called him Home. He was reminiscing about some of his experiences in the ministry. Suddenly he pointed his finger at me and said, "Young man, it won't be long before you will be where I am right now." He told me that the years would fly by swiftly, and that I should keep this in mind as I served the Lord. I was a couple months short of reaching my 47th birthday and hardly thought of myself as middle-aged, but somehow his solemn words made me think of the time that remained as very

9

brief. He was about 27 years older than I, and now as I write, I have used up almost 14 of them.

Yes, the years between 50 and the time of our departure from this world fly by very swiftly. We who are Christians should acknowledge this fact openly and cheerfully. After all, we believe that the home to which we go at death is far better than anything we've ever had here. We also have the assurance that we will reach Heaven the instant we die. Paul made the positive declaration, "For to me to live is Christ, and to die is gain" (Philippians 1:21), and was extremely precise when he said that immediately upon leaving this body we will be "present with the Lord" (2 Corinthians 5:8).

Some believers, however, simply refuse to discuss the matter of their mortality. I have known folks in their eighties who wouldn't talk about the purchase of a burial plot. They just couldn't bring themselves to confront reality. Such people make-believe that death never will come to them. How much happier they would be and how much more gracefully they would grow old if they would face up to life as it is! Just discussing the biblical teaching about death and beyond would help them so much! And they would have a feeling of satisfaction if they would make a will which spells out clearly their desires regarding their estate.

Of course, I'm not suggesting that people

who have entered their senior adult years should think about death all the time or make it the center of all their conversation. That's not normal. Nor does it make one a socially enjoyable person. Some people may talk glibly about death to mask an inner fear. What we should aim for is a willingness to discuss it and an ability to do so without having morbid, depressing thoughts. A Christian who properly faces the reality of departing this life, acknowledging it openly and cheerfully, will not get sour on life or develop a fixation on death and dying.

A RESOLUTE TRUST IN GOD

Humble, resolute trust in the Lord is the second characteristic of a believer who lives triumphantly with the awesome realization that he's going to die. An essential to this poise and optimism is a working faith. We came to God initially by believing on Him. In difficult times we found help when we looked to the Lord and deliberately placed ourselves trustfully in His care and keeping. And, if we are to enjoy serenity in our last years, we must daily read His Word, obey His commandments, commune with Him in prayer, and consciously submit ourselves to Him.

Some time ago a man in his late sixties told me that he could not visit relatives in a rest home because going there depressed him. When he saw people who had strokes or were dying with cancer, he got to wondering about

11

his own death. He said he started developing imaginary symptoms which soon made him a wreck. He claimed he was having such a hard time because he realized that he would soon be the same age as many of the folks who were in such bad shape.

This man professed to be a Christian, but he certainly wasn't exercising his faith. The Scriptures contain scores of promises to the Lord's people. They are given so that we may read them and appropriate them. One of the most assuring of these verses is 1 Corinthians 10:13,

> There hath no temptation taken you but such as is common to man; but God is faithful, who will not permit you to be tempted above that ye are able, but will, with the temptation, also make the way to escape, that ye may be able to bear it (1 Corinthians 10:13).

The Greek word translated "temptation" refers to both *trials* which come from God to purify His children and to *temptations* which come from the devil to seduce them into sinning. Here we have the assurance that God will place a limit upon the severity of the test and that He will provide strength so that we can come through it victoriously.

Thousands of believers have found that the Lord fulfills His promise. I have seen Him do it repeatedly in the lives of people to whom I have ministered. Among them was a woman of about 70 who had a tendency toward being a worrier. She was having some circulation problems, and she said she'd rather die than face an amputation. The day came, however, when the doctors informed her that they had no choice but to carry out the procedure she had dreaded so much. She was terribly upset. But we talked and prayed, and she found peace. She went through the surgery with triumph and returned home with a new ability to trust God. She had found that His grace is sufficient. This new attitude remained with her until the day the Lord took her home.

The Lord Jesus told us that we should not worry about the future. He put it this way: "Be, therefore, not anxious about tomorrow; for tomorrow will be anxious for the things of itself. Sufficient unto the day is its own evil" (Matthew 6:34). While it is perfectly proper to prepare for tomorrow, it is always wrong to become anxious about it. Getting ready for tomorrow includes thinking through what you will do if God takes your mate to Heaven, permits your health to break down, or lets your finances become depleted. Such forethought has great value. But we should not worry. We have the Lord's promise that He will be with us all the way through this world.

This may be an opportune place to say that we can eliminate a common concern about our final illness by making a so-called "living will." If we don't want life-support machines to keep us breathing for weeks or months in a state of unconsciousness or semi-consciousness, we can prepare a notarized document letting our desire be known. The most pertinent paragraph reads as follows: "If there is no reasonable expectation of my recovering from an illness or injury, I request that I be allowed to die in dignity and not be kept alive by heroic measures. I ask that drugs be administered to me only for the relief of pain and not to prolong my earthly life, even if these pain-killing drugs may hasten my death."

A believer can make out this will without any sense of guilt. All you are doing is asking that doctors withhold any medication and life-supporting procedures which do nothing more than prolong a meaningless kind of existence. We are definitely opposed to euthanasia or mercy killing. We do not believe that doctors should ever actively end a human life. But the request expressed in the "living will" asks for no such measures.

Let's not sap our strength, mar our joy, and hurt our testimony by worrying about the suffering or humiliation which may attend our departure from this world. To do so is foolish and wicked.

It is unwise because most of the things we worry about are not likely to happen. Remember, the Lord Jesus may come for His own at any time. And if He doesn't come soon to take us without dying, He may make death an easy experience for most of us. It just doesn't make any sense at all to worry about the future.

Anxiety about dying is also displeasing to the Lord. It indicates a lack of willingness to trust Him. The God who gave His eternal Son to the cruel death of the cross for our salvation must be pained when we show a lack of confidence in Him. He has proven His love in the gift of His Son. He has shown His concern for your present need by giving you the assurance of your salvation. He has given us the privilege of calling Him "Father," and He refers to us as His "sons and daughters."

A dear Christian lady had cancer surgery a few years ago. Although she has a host of physical problems, she told me that God's goodness in fulfilling His promises has been so real these past few years that she has forgotten how to worry. She knows that she may soon become bedridden and go through a time of suffering before she dies. But she isn't anxious about it. She has learned to trust. What a testimony she is to all who know her! By God's grace and with His help you and I can be like her. We can begin by praying, "Lord, help me to trust You the way I should." Then, depending upon Him, and through the power of the indwelling Holy Spirit, we can make every day a day of humble trust and wonderful peace.

AN AWARENESS OF PURPOSE

A third characteristic which should mark every senior adult Christian is an awareness of the fact that God has placed us on earth that we may glorify Him. In 1 Corinthians 10:31 we read, "Whether, therefore, ye eat, or drink, or whatever ye do, do all to the glory of God." We are also to be the means by which others glorify God, for Jesus said, "Let your light so shine before men, that they may see your good works, and glorify your Father, who is in heaven" (Matthew 5:16). A consciousness of this truth may give us comfort with respect to the past and will surely present us with a challenge for the future.

The realization that we are here to glorify God is assuring to believers who have been faithful to the Lord but have never achieved great success in the eyes of their peers. It helps them recognize that some of the little things they did because they loved the Savior were important to God, met His approval, and will be rewarded. Jesus said that a person who gives a cup of water in His name "shall not lose his reward" (Mark 9:41). Though we thought little of them, our kind words and loving deeds pleased God and glorified Him. Through them we fulfilled, at least in part, the purpose for which He created us.

This awareness should also work as a challenge. It provides us with an incentive for the development of personal holiness and the "fruit of the Spirit." Peter was addressing old and young alike when he wrote, "But, as He who hath called you is holy, so be ye holy in all manner of life, because it is written, Be

16

ye holy; for I am holy" (1 Peter 1:15,16). The autumn season of life is a beautiful time to glorify God by growing the fruit of the Spirit— "love, joy, peace, longsuffering, gentleness, goodness, faith, meekness, self-control" (Galatians 5:22,23).

The later years usually give us more time for meditation, prayer, and the reading of the Scriptures. The demands of life are not as great as they were when we were younger. Sexual desire is less intense, and the ambitions of youth have either been achieved or their pursuit abandoned. This is a wonderful season for spiritual development. Therefore, we should not be content just to wait around for death to come or think in terms of living for selfish pleasure. God challenges us to use these years for His glory by growing in likeness to Jesus and in giving ourselves to the doing of His will.

Sad to say, some older Christians seem to forget about their responsibility to glorify God all the way to the end of life. They worked faithfully in the past. But now they resign from every church committee, relinquish their teaching positions, and become mere church attenders. One man told me, "I've done more than my share for over 30 years. It's time for the younger people to step in and take more of the load. I don't have many years left, and I'm going to enjoy them as much as I can."

Now, I don't begrudge rest and relaxation to older people who have worked hard all their lives. They have a right to step out of positions which involve a great deal of responsibility. But I don't like the attitude which seems to say, "I've earned the right to live selfishly."

Every senior adult believer who enjoys relatively good health should be serving the Lord in some capacity. I'm going to discuss ways in which this can be done in a later chapter, but let's remember that we never reach the place where we can please the Lord or glorify Him by living only for ourselves.

On a few occasions I have found older people who use their consciousness of life's brevity as an excuse for sin. This is shocking! A few years ago I received a telephone call from a neighbor lady asking me if I could come over to talk with her and her husband. I was casually acquainted with them, and I knew they had been very active in their church. I was dumbfounded, therefore, when the woman told me that her husband was having an affair with a younger married woman. He was somewhat embarrassed, but tried to justify his conduct by pointing out a number of faults in his partner of many years. I insisted that he was sinning against God, his wife, his children, and the church. Finally he broke into tears and blubbered, "Well, I'm almost 60 years old. I've got only a few years left. I don't care what you or anyone says, I've got to find some enjoyment in them." Nothing I said dissuaded him from carrying out his intentions. He and the younger woman both divorced their mates and married each other. He is now an unhappy and broken man who has lost everything worthwhile.

It's hard to understand such a person. Since I am not God, I can't judge whether or not this man is truly born again. In any case, he has learned that God's Word is true when it declares, "Be not deceived, God is not mocked, for whatever a man soweth, that shall he also reap" (Galatians 6:7).

In summary, to grow old gracefully, we who have reached the senior adult years should openly and cheerfully acknowledge that we are nearing the end of our earthly race. While not by any means obsessed with the thought of dying, we should be able to discuss the subject without becoming morbid or depressed. As we reflect upon the span between us and eternity, we should also walk with the Lord, trusting Him for the difficulties and distresses associated with aging and dying. His written Word gives us many precious promises on which we can rest, promises like the one found in Isaiah,

> And even to your old age I am He; and
> even to gray hairs will I carry you; I have
> made, and I will bear; even I will carry,
> and will deliver you (Isaiah 46:4).

Finally, we should view our mortality in the light of the purpose for which God made us—to glorify Him. We never retire from this calling. Let's fulfill this vocation by making the closing years of life rich in spiritual development and loving service.

2

THAT MIRROR ON THE WALL

The other day a middle-aged lady declared, "If there's anything I hate, it's those full-length triple mirrors in some clothing stores. When I see myself in them, I sometimes get so discouraged that I go home without buying a dress. I guess I view the situation as hopeless and say to myself, 'What's the use?' " I kiddingly told her she probably didn't need a new dress anyway, making light of the matter. Yet I know she is by no means alone in her aversion to these mirrors. I don't like them myself, and I've always thought that we men are far less vain than our female counterparts.

The fact is that most of us who are past the half-century mark don't like everything we see when we stand in front of a mirror or look at a recent photograph. For many people the source of displeasure begins right at the top. Men in my condition are almost blinded by the glare that comes back from shiny skin surrounded by a white fringe. Some middle-aged and older folk are obviously not happy with the color of their hair or they wouldn't change it. Apparently they also detect other problems on top. They wouldn't be buying so many wigs, falls, and hairpieces if they didn't. There are also those facial wrinkles and lines, double chins, and brown age spots. In addition, everything has started to sag, and the extra inches show up where we don't want them. Even our hands and feet show signs of wear and tear.

Your first reaction to these observations may be quite negative. What a depressing way to start a new chapter! I understand your feelings, but I can assure you that you will not become downhearted and discouraged by what follows. Read on and you will feel better about yourself. If you are a Christian, you need not succumb to "the looking-glass blues." In fact, you can view those evidences of physical deterioration as harbingers of a better life, a new body, and a perfect world. Moreover, you can develop a solid loveliness far more enduring and satisfying than the kind which wins beauty contests.

You and I will be able to accept the message of the mirror on the wall with grace, dignity, and good humor if we follow three simple rules which I am about to suggest. First, we must take the faith view, looking upon the signs of aging as tokens of the better life that awaits us in Heaven. Second, we must resist discouragement and make it our aim to look our best. Third, we must seek to develop that inner beauty which brings about outward transformation.

TAKE THE FAITH VIEW

My first suggestion is that when you see those signs of aging you consciously start reflecting upon Heaven and the new body you will receive there. What you observe in the mirror is one of God's ways of showing us that He did not intend this physical frame in which we are now living to be the eternal abode of the soul. The body with which Adam and Eve were created was designed for this earth, not for Heaven. And that was previous to the fall and the resulting curse! Paul sharply contrasted the body God gave Adam with the glorified one we will receive when Jesus comes for us. We read,

> The first man is of the earth, earthy; the second man is the Lord from heaven.
> As is the earthy, such are they also that are earthy; and as is the heavenly, such are they also that are heavenly.
> And as we have borne the image of the earthy, we shall also bear the image of the heavenly (1 Corinthians 15:47-49).

Adam was created with a body which Paul called "earthy." Undoubtedly he and Eve would never have experienced physical deterioration if they had not sinned. It may be that they would have noticed their hair gradually becoming white and their faces appearing more mature. But they would have retained perfect health and the vitality of youth. It may be that the Lord would have solved the overpopulation problem for our planet by translating them into a heavenly body when they reached the age of 1,000 or so. But enough of such conjecture. The fact is that they did sin, and that their fall brought suffering and death into the human family. Therefore, everyone who isn't raptured must either die young or gradually go through the process of aging.

We who know the Lord, however, need not be distressed by this "fact of life." As we observe the telltale signs of advancing years, we ought to see them as reminders that this sin-cursed planet is only our temporary home, and that we are nearing the one which is eternal and perfect. Paul encouraged us to take this faith view when he wrote,

> For our citizenship is in heaven, from which also we look for the Savior, the Lord Jesus Christ,
>   Who shall change our lowly body, that it may be fashioned like His glorious body, according to the working by which He is able even to subdue all things unto Himself (Philippians 3:20,21).

Let's think of Heaven and our glorious resurrection whenever we feel a bit discouraged by the message of the mirror on the wall. Right now we are living in what the apostle Paul called our lowly body. On account of the curse, it is marked by infirmity, suffering, sickness, and aging. In 1 Corinthians 15:42-49 the words "corruption," "dishonor," "weakness," "natural," and "earthy" are used in connection with our physical frame. But these same verses speak of the *new body* we will receive when Jesus the Lord comes again. And the terms "incorruption," "glory," "power," "spiritual," and "heavenly" are used to denote the qualities it will have. Whenever the mirror reveals another indication of time's inexorable march, we must view it as a token of our wonderful future in Heaven.

Just a few weeks ago an aged man whose knees are badly deformed by osteo-arthritis said to me, "Look at these knees. They look terrible and they hurt. But I'm not going to let this get me down. One of these days I'm going to get a brand-new body." He could make this optimistic comment because he took the faith view.

LOOK YOUR BEST

My second suggestion is that believers who see these evidences of aging should keep their body as healthy as they can, dress neatly, and be well-groomed. A Christian makes a serious mistake when he becomes discouraged by the signs of advancing years and decides he might as well be a slob. I am distressed when I encounter people who are slovenly about their clothing, careless about their grooming, and neglectful of their personal hygiene. It is disturbing to see many older Christians allowing themselves to become flabby and obese. I hate to see any man with a 2-or-3 day growth of stubble on his face or a woman whose hair looks like the rats have nested in it. People who look like this are intimating that they are no longer worthwhile, and that's not true. Older citizens can be extremely useful and wonderfully pleasant companions. Taking a defeatist attitude toward life because we don't like what we see in the mirror is wrong. To consider oneself worthless is to do God a disservice. We also cheat our relatives, friends, and neighbors when we decide that we'll just sit around waiting to die. Senior adult years lived this way are a terrible waste.

While we should always try to look our best, we ought to avoid the extreme to which some aging people go in an effort to appear younger than they are. They become obsessed with their battle against every evidence of the advancing years. Most of us have seen those who wear outlandish clothing in an effort to appear youthful. We feel sorry for them, because we know they are only succeeding in presenting themselves as foolish or eccentric.

Now, I am not criticizing people who resort

to hair rinses or coloring agents, wear a hair-piece, or use ointments to bleach out brown age spots. These practices come under the cover of the personal liberty discussed in Romans 14. It is not my right to judge others for what they do about these telltale evidences of advancing years. If they have a healthy and truly Christian attitude toward their aging but like to maintain as youthful an appearance as possible, they have a right to do so.

Perhaps everyone has some areas of sensitivity with respect to his or her appearance. I personally am not bothered by the brown age spots on the back of my hands, my baldness, or my gray fringe. I would find a hairpiece uncomfortable and would be self-conscious about wearing one. But I have good friends who wear them without embarrassment. As far as I'm concerned, using a hair-coloring agent seems to be worth neither the trouble nor the expense. But I am sensitive about developing a paunch. As a result, I do some running, go through an exercise routine almost every day, and use some restraint in eating. I also have a feeling of being unkempt if I don't shave morning and evening. But I have no illusions about my appearance. When I see my reflection in a mirror, I can tell that I'm a 60-year-old man. And I don't mind it.

If we stop to think about it, we can find that the outward evidences of aging have some plus factors. That grandparent image isn't all bad. Little children love grandpas and grandmas. Many young people, even in this era of rapid change, respect the counsel of older people because they know we've done a lot of living. Actually, the years can have a mellowing and softening effect upon our facial features. They register a unique kindness and gentleness which comes only with age and experience. We can have an aura about our appearance that attracts people to us, even if we are afflicted with a crippling disease or a deformity. It seems to me that almost every older person has a number of strong incentives to look his very best.

DEVELOP YOUR INNER BEAUTY

My third suggestion to Christians in their senior adult years is that they seek to develop an inner, spiritual beauty. Through growth in likeness to Jesus Christ we can reflect in our very appearance a deep and enduring loveliness. Christians who submit to the Holy Spirit become loving, joyous, serene, patient, and self-controlled. These are the outward evidences of an inner transformation.

The apostle Peter was aware of the truth that what we are within is revealed on the outside when he penned his admonition to the Christian wives of unsaved men. He urged them to put far more emphasis upon what they were on the inside than on their hairstyle, jewelry, or clothing. He spoke of "a meek and quiet spirit" as an "ornament." Here are his exact words:

In the same manner, ye wives, be in subjection to your own husbands that, if any obey not the word, they also may without the word be won by the behavior of the wives,

While they behold your chaste conduct coupled with fear;

Whose adorning, let it not be that outward adorning of braiding the hair, and of wearing of gold, or of putting on of apparel,

But let it be the hidden man of the heart in that which is not corruptible, even the ornament of a meek and quiet spirit, which is in the sight of God of great price (1 Peter 3:1-4).

Real attractiveness, therefore, is not primarily related to the external. It stems from character. The deepest and most enduring kind of loveliness grows from within like a flower.

The older we are, the more pronounced will be the correspondence between the inner self and the outward appearance. One day when I was with my wife in a supermarket, I noticed an older man take a pornographic magazine from the rack, open it with a smirk on his face, and show it to a youngster I took to be his grandson. The lad was obviously a bit embarrassed, not knowing exactly how to react, and I actually felt sorry for him. But I had a deep feeling of disgust for his elderly companion, for I could see lust and lechery written on his face.

The countenances of many older men and women reveal an inner cynicism and hardness. But the faces of Christians who have walked with the Lord for many years seem to denote the presence of the Holy Spirit within them. They radiate peace, kindness, purity, and gentleness because they have grown these graces as they have walked in fellowship with their Master.

You can often spot an older Christian at a glance. One day in a restaurant I noticed a couple who must have been in their eighties and my first thought was, "They have walked with the Lord for a long time." I couldn't hear much of what they were saying, but I could tell they were discussing something they had heard in a church service. When the waitress came with the food, they bowed their heads and prayed. They were courteous to one another and to the waitress. Just before leaving, the man put down a gospel tract with a tip. They each rose from their seat with some difficulty, but gave the impression of happiness and contentment as they made their way to the cashier. You could tell that they were deeply in love with one another and at peace with God. I pray that if Jesus tarries and I am spared I will transmit with ever-increasing clarity a signal which says that I am a man who's walked with the Lord for a long time.

In conclusion, let's not allow ourselves to be disturbed by what we see in that mirror on the wall. The marks of aging may be there, but they can be viewed as indicators that we are nearing the time of graduation from earth to Heaven. We have lost the glow and physical appeal of youth, but we can still be useful and attractive. And when we submit to the Holy Spirit, the qualities He produces on the inside will be reflected in our deportment and written on our faces.

When I was a young man in seminary, an elderly minister greatly influenced a group of us young men with a lesson in the art of growing old. He reminded us of the challenge before us and urged us to use our strength for God before we would begin to experience the limitations of poor health or old age. Then, pointing to the top of his head and working down his anatomy he said, "Bald, blind, bridge, bulge, and bunions." The pictures I had seen of him in his youthful days indicated that he had been very handsome. But now signs of age were quite evident, and he was nearly blind.

Yet he didn't appear to be discouraged in the slightest. He said he treated his body as the temple of the Holy Spirit by observing good health laws and being well-groomed. He recognized it as only the temporary house for his soul, but he was neither eager to leave it nor reluctant to do so. He simply had placed himself in the hands of the Lord and was ready for whatever God desired. His eyesight was so poor that he could have been declared legally blind, but he didn't complain. He faced up to all the signs of physical deterioration with grace and dignity. So can we!

3

THOSE ACHING BONES

"Oh, my aching bones"! We've all heard this expression spoken with a low moan and a slight chuckle. An adult is suffering as a result of playing too hard in the ball game at the Sunday school picnic. Our response likely as not is a genial reminder, "You'd better remember that you're not as young as you used to be."

Yes, we can laugh about some of the aches and pains that accompany the passing of the years. But we also encounter a lot of suffering that is not a laughing matter. We don't make humorous remarks when we observe deep distress on the face of a loved one or friend who is critically ill. Quips don't come to our lips when we grope for something to say to a friend suffering with bone cancer. Nor do we feel like joking when we visit an acquaintance who is totally paralyzed, hopelessly senile, or woefully deranged. In the geriatric section of hospitals or the bed care area in nursing homes you can see sights and hear sounds which may make falling asleep a difficult chore for you. Or you may be rudely awakened by their reappearing in a nightmare.

Suffering can accompany any period of our earthly sojourn, but it is usually more prominent during our senior adult years. We will either experience it in our own bodies, or confront it in someone we love very much. And learning how to cope with it is an important element in the art of growing old.

C. S. Lewis in his *The Problem of Pain* and Philip Yancey in his *Where Is God When It Hurts?* have presented comprehensive Christian studies of human suffering, and I'm not going to duplicate what they have written. Instead, I will focus our attention upon the infirmities and illnesses usually associated with aging.

I believe I am qualified to write about this subject because I have entered my sixth decade and have counseled literally hundreds of the elderly who are suffering and dying. I am firmly convinced that those who have entered the years when infirmities multiply and pains increase cannot enjoy peace and serenity without the reality of the Christian hope. Therefore, we must begin by making sure we have accepted the Lord Jesus as our

Savior. Then we should seek to apply the truths of God's Word to daily living, which will enable us to go through our last years with grace and dignity.

We must begin by gaining an understanding of the nature and extent of the curse God placed upon the earth because of sin. Second, we must comprehend the doctrine of God's sovereignty and apply it to our own particular situation. Third, we must clearly recognize the role of faith in the life of God's children and find God to be real as we exercise it.

THE NATURE AND EXTENT OF THE CURSE

First, afflicted saints must see that the basic reason for most of their suffering goes back to the curse God pronounced upon the earth immediately after Adam and Eve sinned. If we understand this biblical truth, we will not add to our distress by torturing ourselves with the thought that some wrong in our lives accounts for our pain.

The story of the fall of Adam and Eve is recorded in the opening chapters of the Bible. God placed our first parents in the garden of Eden and told them they could eat all the fruit except that which grew on the tree of the knowledge of good and evil. He warned them that if they disobeyed they would die. But disobey they did. The Bible tells us they immediately felt a sense of guilt which caused them to make clothing for themselves out of fig leaves. Then when they heard a sound indicating that the Lord was coming to speak with them, they hid among the trees. God found them, however, and called them to account. He showed His grace to Adam and Eve by promising redemption through "the seed of the woman." Then He told them that from this point on they and their descendants would live out their days as fallen human beings on a cursed earth. We read,

> Unto the woman He said, I will greatly multiply thy sorrow and thy conception; in sorrow thou shalt bring forth children; and thy desire shall be to thy husband, and he shall rule over thee.
>
> And unto Adam He said, Because thou hast hearkened unto the voice of thy wife, and hast eaten of the tree, of which I commanded thee, saying, Thou shalt not eat of it: cursed is the ground for thy sake; in sorrow shalt thou eat of it all the days of thy life;
>
> Thorns also and thistles shall it bring forth to thee; and thou shalt eat the herb of the field;
>
> In the sweat of thy face shalt thou eat bread, till thou return unto the ground; for out of it wast thou taken: for dust thou art, and unto dust shalt thou return (Genesis 3:16-19).

Human sinfulness, which brought our planet under God's curse, is the root cause of hurricanes, tornados, earthquakes, floods, periods of drought, unbearable heat, and deadly cold, along with noxious plants, injurious insects, venomous serpents, and ravenous beasts. The sentence of physical death for mankind is the origin of diseases like cancer, hardening of the arteries, multiple sclerosis, tuberculosis, diabetes, and the like. Moreover, every accident and crime is a reminder that we are fallen creatures who live in an imperfect, inharmonious world.

An understanding that the curse is the reason for most human suffering ought to be a great help to us when we are afflicted. It assures us that our suffering is not necessarily related to a special sin on our part. It helps us realize that diseases like cancer do not come as personal punishment but simply as the means by which God will take us from this world.

I love the calm attitude of a middle-aged believer who was stricken with a fast-moving cancer which he knew would take him very quickly. He looked at us without any show of emotion and said, "We all live under the sentence of physical death, and this just happens to be the way I'm going to die. I'm not surprised because my parents both died the same way. And I'm not afraid. I know that I'm a member of God's family through faith in Christ and that I'll soon be Home."

If we have arthritis and the pain is especially intense because the weather is humid, we must not think God has forsaken us or that He is punishing us. This combination of factors is a natural phenomenon. It is the consequence of our living as fallen human beings upon this cursed planet.

True, the Lord often speaks to us through affliction. And on some occasions He brings it into our lives because we have sinned. In 1 Corinthians 11:30, for example, we are told that some of the early Christians were weak and sickly because of carelessness in their observance of the Lord's Supper. But when the Lord does chasten through illness or pain, He makes it clear to us through the ministry of the Holy Spirit. He doesn't want us feeling guilty every time we suffer.

The Lord Jesus took great pains to correct the thinking of His disciples on this matter. They saw a man who had been blind from birth and asked, "Master, who did sin, this man, or his parents?" In response our Lord answered, "Neither hath this man sinned, nor his parents, but that the works of God should be made manifest in him" (John 9:2,3). Our Lord apparently didn't think it necessary to tell the apostles that ultimately all suffering is traceable to the fall of Adam and Eve. Nor did He acknowledge that sin in parents can produce a disease like syphilis which in turn can cause the birth of a physically or mentally handicapped infant. He simply declared that no particular sin was responsible for this man's condition and assured them that this misfortune provided an opportunity for the work of God to be demonstrated.

If we keep the truth of the fall in mind, we won't take a guilt trip every time we become sick or experience pain. We will realize that original sin is the reason we suffer in the aging process. Actually, we will view these indicators of physical deterioration as hopeful signs. They give notice that the time of our release from all the effects of sin is drawing near.

THE SOVEREIGNTY OF GOD

A second theological truth every suffering saint ought to grasp clearly is that of God's absolute sovereignty. The older we grow the more we should appreciate the fact that He is the absolute owner and ruler of everything. He created the universe out of nothing for His glory, and He has been keeping it intact ever since He made it.

The theological textbooks on my shelf contain fine discussions of God's sovereignty, but some of the material is quite heavy. Therefore, I'm not going to try to summarize what they say. Instead, I'm going to quote a brief definition I came across recently in a non-theological book written by Peg Rankin. It was formulated by a young man working for his doctorate in physics who said, "God can do any thing He wants to do, any time He wants to do it, any way He wants to do it, and for any purpose He wants to accomplish." (*Yet Will I Trust Him,* page 23, G-L Publications, Regal Books Division, Glendale, California, 1980.) That's the clearest statement about God's sovereignty I've ever seen!

This power and authority of God is beautifully expressed in the Scriptures. Listen to the words of the psalmist: "But our God is in the heavens; He hath done whatsoever He hath pleased" (Psalm 115:3). King Nebuchadnezzar, upon coming back to his throne after a period of insanity, waxed eloquent when he said,

> I blessed the Most High, and I praised and honored Him who liveth forever, whose dominion is an everlasting dominion, and His kingdom is from generation to generation.
>
> And all the inhabitants of the earth are reputed as nothing; and He doeth according to His will in the army of heaven, and among the inhabitants of the earth, and none can stay His hand, or say unto Him, What doest Thou?
>
> Now I, Nebuchadnezzar, praise and extol and honor the King of heaven, all whose works are truth, and His ways justice; and those that walk in pride He is able to abase (Daniel 4:34,35,37).

I am convinced that we must bow to God's absolute right to do what He wants to do. So I am going to include still another Bible passage dealing with the subject of His sovereignty—Romans 9.

In this chapter we find Paul's answer to the objection of some Jewish believers that God wasn't being fair to them in allowing Gentiles to have equal status in the church. The apostle first reminded them of the Lord's choice of Isaac over Ishmael and Jacob over Esau. He knew they would agree that the Almighty had a perfect right to choose Isaac and Jacob as the channels through whom He would bring salvation to mankind. He then reminded them of another historical person, Pharaoh, the Egyptian ruler who didn't want to let the Israelites leave his land. God could have caused this monarch to capitulate through fear, but instead the Almighty gave him the courage to stand by his wrong decision. Thus the Lord made Pharaoh an object lesson for all mankind.

Did God have a right to choose Isaac over Ishmael and Jacob over Esau? Did He have a right to use Pharaoh as an example of what happens to those who resist Him? Did He have a right to give Gentiles equality with the Jews in the church? Does the Lord have a right to show more mercy to some people than others? Here is Paul's answer to those who dare say no:

> Nay but, O man, who art thou that repliest against God? Shall the thing formed say to him that formed it, Why hast thou made me thus?
>
> Hath not the potter power over the

clay, of the same lump to make one vessel unto honor, and another unto dishonor?

What if God, willing to show His wrath and to make His power known, endured with much longsuffering the vessels of wrath fitted to destruction;

And that He might make known the riches of His glory on the vessels of mercy, which He had before prepared unto glory,

Even us, whom He hath called, not of the Jews only, but also of the Gentiles? (Romans 9:20-24).

God is not answerable to man. We act in sinful pride whenever we try to pass judgment upon Him. Remember, "God can do any thing He wants to do, any time He wants to do it, any way He wants to do it, and for any purpose He wants to accomplish."

The doctrine of God's sovereignty is of tremendous practical importance. If we believe it, we will be able to endure pain and distress without a trace of rebellion. We won't fall into the helpless despair of those who think in terms of a blind fate. We will rest assured that our affliction is not the result of Satan's gaining the upper hand. We will have a healthy attitude toward the matter of healing.

Sovereignty and Fate

A person who understands the biblical doctrine of God's sovereignty will never fall into a fatalistic attitude or become stoical in his responses. Affirming that a holy, all-powerful, all-wise, and loving God can do any thing He wants to do any time He wants to do it, any way He wants to do it, for whatever purpose He wants to accomplish is a far cry from "what will be, will be." A Christian who has cried to God in his distress but has not received deliverance can rest in the assurance that his pain is not an accident of fate nor a tragedy. It has been permitted by a God who is too holy to do anything wrong, too powerful to be overcome by hostile forces, too wise to make a mistake, and too loving to do anything unkind.

Let's believe and apply the wonderful truth of God's sovereignty! It assures us that nothing comes into our lives as an accident without purpose. It tells us that we are never the victims of a blind fate. Thus it enables us to avoid the dour pessimism and hopeless resignation so often characteristic of older folks.

I must confess that I am sometimes shaken when I see aged Christians dying by inches and completely out of touch with reality. I find myself wondering why the Lord doesn't take them Home. I even plead with Him to do so. But I am consoled by a deep conviction that the sovereign Lord who has permitted these sad situations has done so for a good reason.

Recently I received a telephone call from an elderly lady whose husband is a helpless invalid in a rest home. She is not in the best of health herself, and visiting him regularly drains her strength. A series of strokes have taken away his ability to communicate. He appears to recognize her, but he doesn't seem to know anyone else. It breaks our hearts to see this once robust and active man. It seems to us that it would have been far better for him and his family if the Lord had taken him with one massive stroke rather than allowing a series of small ones to reduce him to this state. But as soon as I start thinking this way, I remind myself that I'm not God. Figuratively, I put my hand to my mouth so I won't speak a proud or rebellious word. I acknowledge that the Lord knows what is best. I also reaffirm my conviction that He has a right to do whatever He wants to do, in any way He wants to do it, any time He wants to do it, and for whatever purpose He wishes to accomplish. Then, having acknowledged God's sovereignty, I experience the comforting and confirming ministry of the Holy Spirit. I am assured anew that God's grace will prove sufficient for all involved in this difficult situation. I know that good will come from it because I believe Romans 8:28. The biblical doctrine of God's sovereignty is not to be equated with fatalism. It is a tremendously practical and comforting truth.

Sovereignty and Satan

If we understand the doctrine of God's

sovereignty, we will never fall into the trap of thinking that Satan may have gotten the upper hand in our lives. It is surprising how many Christians are confused on this score. Some Bible teachers promote the idea that God wants everybody well all the time and that He would keep people this way except for two problems. Sometimes people violate His natural laws. And sometimes the devil gets his own way.

Now, to the best of my knowledge, everybody agrees that we can harm our bodies by abusing them and by violating laws of good health. It is also true that Satan had a hand in Job's suffering, and that the apostle Paul spoke of his "thorn in the flesh" as "the messenger of Satan to buffet me" (2 Corinthians 12:7). But the Scriptures never indicate that God wants everybody well all the time or that He ever loses control over the devil.

In refuting these wrong ideas, let's start with the teaching that God wants everybody well all the time. This is an attractive concept, but it simply isn't true. The apostle Paul underscored this repeatedly in his epistles. In 2 Corinthians 12 he referred to his "thorn in the flesh" as an affliction by the will of God. Three times he asked God to remove this physical malady, but instead of receiving his request, the Lord gave him the message, "My grace is sufficient for thee; for My strength is made perfect in weakness" (2 Corinthians 12:9).

When the apostle discovered that it was God's will for him to have this affliction, he concluded, "Most gladly, therefore, will I rather glory in my infirmities, that the power of Christ may rest upon me. Therefore, I take pleasure in infirmities, in reproaches, in necessities, in persecutions, in distresses for Christ's sake; for when I am weak, then am I strong" (2 Corinthians 12:9,10).

The devil was involved in this experience only in trying to harass the apostle through it. But the good purpose for which the Lord had brought this bodily infirmity into Paul's life was accomplished. He learned to depend wholly upon the Lord, and this gave him strength he could never have had on his own.

In writing to the Christians in Thessalonica, Paul told them they should not lose heart at the troubles through which they were passing, because "yourselves know that *we are appointed to these things.* For verily, when we were with you, we told you before that we should suffer tribulation, even as it came to pass, and ye know" (1 Thessalonians 3:3,4).

This same apostle also spoke positively about affliction in his letter to the believers in Colosse. Referring to his own distresses, he wrote, "Who now rejoice in my sufferings for you, and fill up that which is behind of the afflictions of Christ in my flesh for His body's sake, which is the church" (Colossians 1:24). Some Bible scholars interpret these words to mean that the Lord Jesus has left behind for

His people a quota of suffering which is essential to the carrying out of His purposes. Others say that though Christ's payment for sin was accomplished "once for all," He still suffers when His followers do, and that our pain is the completion of His suffering. Regardless of which of these interpretations we accept, we are assured that pain and affliction are within the will of God for His people. Don't believe anyone who says that it is God's will for everyone to be well all the time.

The other claim is that some Christians are ill contrary to the will of God because Satan has gained temporary control of the situation. That's preposterous! The Bible teaches us that Satan can afflict a believer only to the degree that God permits. In the story of Job, the Lord first told Satan, "Behold, all that he hath is in thy power; only upon himself put not forth thine hand" (Job 1:12). The devil caused the patriarch to lose all his possessions, even his children. The evil one then complained that he couldn't give Job a thorough test unless he could afflict him with bodily pain. In response, God said, "Behold, he is in thine hand; but save his life" (Job 2:6). The enemy now could afflict Job with dreadful pain, but he could not bring about the patriarch's death. He and his demonic assistants can afflict us only to the extent of God's sovereign permission. The Almighty sets the limit. This assurance can be a source of great comfort to a suffering saint.

Sovereignty and Healing

Another mistaken concept which needs correcting is the idea that our lack of faith may keep God from healing us. Some Bible teachers declare that our Lord's atonement provided for the present healing of the body as well as salvation. They say that the faith of some people is strong enough to save their souls but not to bring about their physical healing. This teaching has brought untold distress to many sincere Christians. In addition to their physical pain, they suffer from a feeling of guilt. They are convinced that their sinful lack of faith is preventing their healing.

To demolish this false teaching, let me begin by considering the claim that the present healing of our bodies was provided in the atonement. Here is the proof text used by those who take this position.

> When the evening was come, they brought unto Him many that were possessed with demons; and He cast out the spirits with His word, and healed all that were sick,
>
> That it might be fulfilled which was spoken by Isaiah, the prophet, saying, He Himself took our infirmities, and bore our sicknesses (Matthew 8:16,17).

You will observe that Matthew did indeed say, "He Himself took our infirmities, and bore our sicknesses." And the Old Testament passage does read: "He hath borne our griefs, and carried our sorrows," and "with His stripes we are healed" (Isaiah 53:4,5). But the healing of which they spoke has to do with our ultimate deliverance from pain and death when we receive our glorified bodies. Matthew referred to our Lord's healing ministry as a sign of His coming to provide *both* forgiveness from the penalty of sin *and* deliverance from all its effects. His healings pointed to the fact that the body of humiliation, though subject to disease and death, is going to be transformed and glorified. The temporary healings were pointers to their future perfection through rapture or resurrection.

The very fact that Christians down through the centuries have become ill and died is in itself a refutation of the idea that the present healing of the body is included in the atonement. If it were, every saint since the day of Pentecost should have escaped death. Christians should have been raptured one by one or allowed to remain on earth until the time Jesus comes for His own.

The proponents of immediate healing on the basis of the atonement die from illnesses and accidents just like the rest of humanity. Did this divine provision lose its efficacy at some point in their lives? No, the substitutionary death of Christ paid the full penalty for sin and the resurrection broke the power of death, but we must still participate in the discomfort, grief, and pain associated with aging.

In summary, let's reaffirm our confidence

that all healing as well as all sickness is under the control of our sovereign God. He has the right to give some people better health than others. He has the power to bring healing from any affliction He permits, but He has no obligation to make us well whether it be through natural or supernatural means. Therefore, when we are suffering from a bodily ailment from which He does not bring us a speedy deliverance, we must not doubt His goodness or might. Nor may we permit a spirit of rebellion to gain a foothold in our lives.

Remember, God's right to do *any thing* He wants to do includes permitting you to experience pain. His right to do what He wants to do *any time* and in *any way* He wants to do it includes healing you suddenly, gradually—or not at all. And His right to do what He wants for *any purpose* He has in mind includes using suffering to develop your Christian character and to bring glory to Himself. Remember, He's God.

THE FUNCTION OF FAITH

A third important theological truth every suffering saint should understand is that of the function of faith. Trust in God lies at the very heart of biblical Christianity. In order to become a member of the family of the redeemed, we must take a step of faith. We continue the Christian life in day-by-day trust and obedience. As we do, we experience increasingly the reality of His presence and power.

All approach to God is an act of faith. We read, ". . . that cometh to God must *believe* that He is, and that He is a rewarder of them that diligently seek Him" (Hebrews 11:6). The apostle Paul wrote, "For by grace are ye saved through *faith*; and that not of yourselves, it is the gift of God—not of works, lest any man should boast" (Ephesians 2:8,9). And in Hebrews 11:7-40 we find a long list of men and women who pleased God and accomplished great exploits through *faith*.

It is obvious, therefore, that God places great value upon believing Him. He works in such a way that only those who have the eyes of faith can perceive Him clearly in nature and in human history. Only believers can experience the truths of the Bible. And God wants us to believe on Him as a moral choice. He has therefore withheld tangible, scientific proofs for His existence. But if He were to give perfect health, great success, tremendous popularity, and long life to everyone who believes on Him, He would provide evidence for His existence which would make faith unnecessary. People would bow to Him simply because they would be convinced that doing so pays in the here-and-now. The Lord would not be glorified through that kind of belief.

God will not make cosmic pets out of His children. He allows us to suffer the same distresses as the wicked around us. True, our lifestyle may keep us from contracting venereal diseases or prevent liver damage and other ills of alcohol. But apart from these, we can expect that we will suffer the same physical distresses as the unsaved and die from the same causes.

Job proved the reality of his faith by continuing to trust God even after he had lost everything that had made his life enjoyable. Sitting on an ash heap, suffering from skin ulcers which made him repulsive to even his wife and best friends, he could say, "Though He slay me, yet will I trust in Him" (Job 13:15). And when he despaired of showing his peers that no special sin on his part had caused this affliction, he could still make the affirmation, "For I know that my Redeemer liveth, and that He shall stand at the latter day upon the earth; and though after my skin worms destroy this body, yet in my flesh shall I see God" (Job 19:25,26). After confessing that he couldn't understand God's ways, he added, "But He knoweth the way that I take; when He hath tested me, I shall come forth as gold" (Job 23:10).

The apostle Paul also possessed this implicit confidence in God. He was in a damp, cold dungeon awaiting execution. He had come to the conclusion that God was not going to deliver him from the headsman's sword. But his faith didn't waver. Instead, he broke forth with an eloquent expression of implicit trust.

> For I am now ready to be offered, and the time of my departure is at hand.
>
> I have fought a good fight, I have finished my course, I have kept the faith;
>
> Henceforth there is laid up for me a crown of righteousness, which the Lord, the righteous judge, shall give me at that day; and not to me only, but unto all them also that love His appearing (2 Timothy 4:6-8).

As we grow older, we are likely to encounter an increase of pain and sorrow. Afflictions will test our faith, but we need not be dismayed. In 1 Corinthians 10:13 we are assured that God will not permit us to be tempted above our ability to withstand and that He will give us all the grace we need. In the meantime, let's exercise our faith, trusting the Lord day-by-day for all the little things which tend normally to upset us. Let's walk in continual fellowship with God, casting our cares upon Him. Just as our muscles grow stronger through use, so faith increases in strength as it is exercised.

A few years ago, I saw the value of daily trust in the life of a Christian man whom I had known from my teenage years. I appreciated the encouragement he gave me when I began speaking at street meetings and in jail services. He assured me of his prayers as I left for the service during World War II. I had a few contacts with him during the years that followed. Always, from the very beginning of our friendship, I saw him as a man who walked with God. This was still true during his closing days as a terminally ill patient in a rest home. I found him emaciated and disfigured, but lucid and happy in the Lord. He was so weak that I visited only briefly, shared a few verses of Scripture with him, and prayed. I left the room thankful for the reality of God's presence in the life of this dying man.

That's not the end of the story, however. As I walked into the hall, a nurse recognized me and bubbled with enthusiasm as she told me about this man's witness. She said that when he was admitted he was well enough to be placed in a wheelchair. During this period of time they had often taken him from room to room so that he might minister to others. Later, when he was too weak to be moved from his room, folks were wheeled in to his bedside. Scores of people received spiritual help from him. Some were saved. As I listened, I couldn't help but think of the fact that this godly man's lifelong walk paid great dividends. He died a glowing witness.

Christian friend, just as your eyes are the physical organs by which you see the natural world, faith is the spiritual organ by which you can be brought in touch with the invisible. God manifests Himself to those who trust Him. Hebrews 11:1 reads, "Now faith is the substance of things hoped for, the evidence of things not seen." This verse confirms what we have just said. It assures us that faith gives substance to our hopes and makes us certain of the realities we cannot see with our physical eyes. Learn now to trust God. You will discover the truth of 1 John 5:4, ". . . and this is the victory that overcometh the world, even our faith."

4
THAT "OVER THE HILL" FEELING

It is interesting to observe the reactions of people when they begin a new decade. One of our friends recently spoke with such a feeling of dread about her 30th birthday that some of us decided to surprise her with a party. We gave her a box of prunes, a bottle of liniment, a jar of Esoterica, and other "appropriate" gifts.

Another woman said that when she reached her 40th birthday she was so overwhelmed with the thought of everything going downhill that she had a long talk with her husband and sought counsel from her pastor.

A successful businessman who reached the half-century mark masked his feelings quite well but kept saying, "Just think, I'm two-thirds of the way through life. I'm only 15 years from retirement, and I can already see some of the younger fellows moving ahead of me."

These negative reactions to certain birthdays contain one common element—an "over the hill" feeling. Some women are distraught because they suddenly realize they have passed the apex of youthful beauty. Men often begin to worry about losing their virility. Some people start thinking about the dreams and aspirations of younger years and realize they will never attain them. They are now on the downward side.

Many men and women succumb to this "over the hill" complex. That's why you see some folks in their forties talking, walking, and acting like they are pushing a hundred and ten. They continue in their daily tasks, but that's about all. If they are asked to expend a little energy on an extra curricular project, they are likely to beg off. A common response is: "Oh no! I can't do that. I'm getting too old." They enclose themselves in a shell and live selfishly. And this is a sure path to misery!

Happily, not everyone takes this defeatist attitude toward the middle and later decades of life. On the contrary, many insist that these years can be the most productive of all, viewing the experiences they've had as an asset. They may even quote with approval Browning's well-known words: "Grow old along with me. The best is yet to be. The last of life for which the first was made."

True, the middle and senior adult years are

57

traumatic for many people. Some lose their mates during this time. Lately, folks who have been married many years are encountering serious marital problems and getting divorces. Loss of health begins to plague some men and women. Parents in this age bracket are sometimes ignored by their grown sons and daughters. Forced retirement may bring about financial stress and other difficulties.

These changes in marital status, health, family relationships, and finances can give middle-aged and older people a sense of insecurity and a low estimate of personal worth. They start feeling unneeded and useless. And in this chapter I'm going to address myself to these problems. I have five simple suggestions which I hope will be helpful to everyone between 41 and 101.

READJUST YOUR GOALS

First, men and women who are depressed because they see themselves as "over the hill" should examine their goals and readjust them if necessary. This is a healthy exercise for every believer regardless of age or status.

This evaluation of goals and priorities is imperative for middle-aged men and women who have been successful but are overwhelmed with a sense of emptiness. As they reflect upon the swiftly passing years and realize that their exit from life is nearer than the time of their entrance into it, they are troubled. They know they have not grown spiritually and have not been laying up treasure in Heaven. In their dissatisfaction with their accomplishments, they automatically engage in healthy introspection. This will lead to some good readjustments in goals and priorities.

Now, this process of self-examination and rectification doesn't follow exactly the same course with every person. For some, putting Christ first may mean leaving a lucrative position and going into the Lord's work at a far lower salary. For others, it may not result in such a radical change of lifestyle.

A middle-aged man who was doing well as a salesman told me one day that he wasn't finding his work satisfying, and that he wondered if he should change jobs. During his earlier years he found that making money was all the incentive he needed. But lately he said he had been thinking about the influence he would leave behind him if the Lord should suddenly take him to Heaven. He was getting less and less satisfaction from his work. At the end of the day he would tell himself, "Well, you've convinced a couple of firms to buy your product rather than one of the competing brands. Big deal!" I could tell that he was genuinely concerned about putting the Lord first in his life. We agreed that he should contact a number of Christian organizations to see if they could use his talents and services as a field representative or fund raiser. He did, and he found that his qualifications were almost perfect for an available position. He is now working for a mission agency for very little financial remuneration. But he is happy and feels fulfilled.

Of course, not all middle-aged people are led into what we call "full-time Christian service." Many men and women doing secular work are exactly where the Lord wants them. They may sometimes become a bit discouraged with their tasks. They may wonder how much glory their work is bringing to God. But when such thoughts come, they need to remind themselves that tool and die makers, typists, computer operators, assembly line workers, and construction people all fill an important role in society. Moreover, they can glorify God in everything they do.

All of us need to acknowledge that the kind of person we are is more important than what we have accomplished. If we walk with the Lord and develop the fruit of the Spirit, we can make a great impact for Christ wherever we go. How we use our money and how we spend our spare time is tremendously significant. Actually, some men and women who hold secular positions have been among the Lord's most fruitful servants.

Let's all evaluate our goals and make the adjustments necessary to give Jesus Christ first place in our lives. We can be assured that the Lord will direct us if we truly seek His wisdom. And when we obey His command to "seek. . . first the kingdom of God and His righteousness," we will not be plagued by that "over the hill" feeling.

BE FAMILY ORIENTED

Second, middle-aged men and women can counter their sense of emptiness or uselessness by placing a high premium upon their family relationships. A person deeply involved with his loved ones will not feel unneeded or useless.

Men and women who still have their mates should try to strengthen the sense of "togetherness" which is essential in a good marriage. All too often a man and his wife tend to drift apart during these years. They stop communicating and go their separate ways. Many folks who have been married for 30 or 40 years are ending their relationship in a divorce court. This is a tragedy! But almost equally heartbreaking are those situations in which two people live together under one roof without warmth and tender love. Both parties feel they are "over the hill." The wife develops this complex because she thinks she is no longer sexually attractive to her husband. The man sees his lack of sexual desire as an indication that he is losing his manhood. Neither seems to realize that this change from younger years is more psychological than physical.

A man and woman living together this way should not look upon their situation as normal. Nor should they go to the opposite extreme and buy sex manuals or try to stimulate sexual desire by looking at pornographic books and films. They should accept a lessening of the sexual drive as normal and avoid becoming preoccupied with this thought. A husband and wife who communicate, read the Bible together, pray with one another, and develop common interests will almost always have a satisfactory sexual life. Even in the senior adult years.

One of the beauties of a deepening marital relationship is a comfortable togetherness. A husband and wife should enjoy being together and feel relaxed even when neither says anything. They are not under a burden to keep conversation going all the time. Judy Paris penned these observations of an older couple sitting opposite her in a restaurant and finishing their meal:

> His wife seemed not to notice anything he was doing, lost still in her own thoughts as her eyes wandered about the room. Yet, she rose from the table in unison with him.
>
> They still did not speak as they pushed their chairs gently toward the table and prepared to leave, she in front of him, he slowly reaching for his cane and holding check and wallet. Just then his knee brushed the corner of a chair and he stumbled, ever so slightly.
>
> "Be careful, be careful, Papa," she said,

and her arm reached out should he fall. He was quick to reassure her.

"I'm okay, Mama, let's go," and he slipped his arm around her waist, still clutching his check and wallet.

They moved slowly to the cashier's counter, and I realized that these two were very much together. (Judy Paris, "Very Much Together" *Home Life,* October 1974, p. 9.)

Husbands and wives who do not nurture their relationship to make it rich and sweet during their later decades are cheating themselves out of one of life's greatest blessings. We who still have our mates should be deeply grateful for them and with God's help make our last years together the best of all.

The exhortation to develop close ties goes beyond the husband-wife relationship. It includes parents and offspring. This is important for couples, but even more so for men and women who have lost their mates. I know that sometimes sons and daughters are wayward, and I realize that they do not always reciprocate the love their parents show them.

In fact, some lonely and afflicted older people have told me bitterly that they have troubles enough of their own without taking on those of their children. I doubt if these parents really mean what they are saying. They are only expressing the feelings they have at the moment. But no parent should even consider taking this attitude. We should do our best to maintain contact with our sons and daughters and never give up praying for them. It seems to me that we will never feel unneeded and useless as long as we know that God can use our prayers in the lives of our sons and daughters.

Sometimes middle-aged people who are themselves grandparents have a father or mother for whom they are still responsible. If so, they must not forget Ephesians 6:2,3, "Honor thy father and mother (which is the first commandment with promise), that it may be well with thee, and thou mayest live long on the earth." The Lord gives us a pledge of His blessing if we obey this commandment.

Recently my wife and I saw four women coming out of a restaurant. They all bore a family resemblance, and my wife said, "I'll bet they represent four generations." I'm almost sure she was right. I guessed their ages as about 20, 40, 65, and 85. We were impressed with the tenderness the second oldest woman was showing toward her aged mother. All four appeared to enjoy being together. I said to my wife, "When that 65-year-old lady reaches old age, she'll probably be treated with the same love she is showing to her mother."

Joy Davidman tells a touching story which underscores the point that we not only please God but also help ourselves when we show kindness toward our aging loved ones. She wrote:

Once upon a time there was a little old man. His eyes blinked and his hands trembled. When he ate, he clattered the silverware distressingly, missed his mouth with the spoon as often as not, and dribbled a bit of his food on the tablecloth. Now he lived with his married son, having nowhere else to live, and his son's wife was a modern young woman who knew that in-laws should not be tolerated in a woman's home.

"I can't have this," she exclaimed. "It interferes with a woman's right to happiness."

So she and her husband took the little old man gently but firmly by the arm and led him to the corner of the kitchen. There they sat him on a stool and gave him his food, what there was of it, in an earthenware bowl. From then on he always ate in the corner, blinking at the table with wistful eyes.

One day his hands trembled rather more than usual, and the earthenware bowl fell and broke.

"If you are a pig," said the daughter-in-law, "you must eat out of a trough." So they made him a little wooden trough and he got his meals in that way.

These people had a 4-year-old son of whom they were very fond. One suppertime the young man noticed his boy playing intently with some bits of wood and asked what he was doing.

"I'm making a trough," he said, smiling up for approval, "to feed you and mamma out of when I get big."

The man and his wife looked at each other for a while and didn't say anything. Then they cried a little. Then they went to the corner and took the little old man by the arm and led him back to the table. They sat him in a comfortable chair and gave him his food on a plate, and from then on nobody ever scolded when he clattered or spilled or broke things. (Joy Davidman, *Smoke on the Mountain,* Philadelphia, Westminster Press, 1953, pp. 60-61.)

The importance of developing a close relationship with our loved ones cannot be over-emphasized. Caring for one another and knowing that others care for us are tremendous antidotes for that "over the hill" feeling.

CULTIVATE A WIDE RANGE OF CONCERN

Third, we can do much to feel needed and wanted by taking a keen interest in people everywhere. We come into direct contact with fellow human beings in our neighborhood, at work, and in church. We hear about God's servants, some of whom labor in difficult places and need our prayers. Through the news media we are continually reminded of the masses of mankind everywhere. We have varying degrees of responsibility toward all of them, and in fulfilling this obligation we will find both joy and satisfaction.

Our concern should begin in our neighborhood. Many of us live near folks who are lonely or poor or infirm. We may know a young couple who would go to a church function if someone would offer free babysitting. A divorcee whose heart has been broken by an unfaithful husband may need the friendship of a motherly Christian woman. An aged widow who can't drive might love to get out once in a while to do some shopping. No senior adult who goes out of his way to show kindness to such folks will feel unneeded or useless.

Just being a warm, helpful, and friendly person pays great dividends in self-esteem. I saw this in one of my uncles. He married late in life and therefore didn't have any children. But he was a friend to all the boys and girls in his neighborhood. When he retired from his factory job, he mowed the grass for several older people who couldn't do it for themselves and were trying to get by on a small fixed income. He repaired screen doors and did other little jobs free of charge. He allowed the youngsters to play in his yard. Everybody thought of him as a happy and fulfilled man. When the Lord took him home, many boys and girls from the neighborhood visited the funeral home to pay their respects. They cried as they viewed his body in the casket.

Another area of ministry for middle-aged people involves missionaries. Folks who have retired can write letters. They shouldn't expect a personal reply. (However, the missionaries will often pen a few words as a postscript on a form letter.) Almost everyone in the Lord's service deeply appreciates Christians who take an interest in their work and will share their prayer concerns. And a believer who is actively engaged in such a ministry of help will never become overwhelmed with a feeling of uselessness.

In short, we need not be depressed by the thought that we have lost our usefulness. We may see young folks stepping into the roles we once filled. We may find it necessary to cut down in certain areas of life. But we need not be unprofitable Christian citizens. The world is full of people who will be greatly cheered by a few kind words or a helpful deed. Even if our health deteriorates to such an extent that we can do nothing more than pray, we can still enjoy the satisfaction of knowing that we are filling a role in the service of God and our fellowmen.

BE A CHURCH MEMBER

Being a good church member is still another way we can counteract that "over the hill" feeling. I have chosen the adjective "good" rather than "active." I did this because some people who can no longer serve on a committee or work on a project can still be valuable members of a church. Their health may keep them from attending regularly, but they can be testimonies to God's grace and effective prayer warriors.

For Christians who are blessed with good health, the middle and later adult years provide wonderful opportunities to serve God in the local church. During this timespan they are free from the responsibilities and restrictions of parenthood. They are no longer utilizing their evenings "moonlighting" for a little extra income, remodeling a house, or repairing an old jalopy. They now have a chance to work for the Lord's cause, to do things for which they didn't have time during their younger years. But sad to say, many believers don't seem to think in terms of eternal riches. They make Sunday a *holiday* instead of a *holy day*. They spend so many weekends away that they cannot teach a Sunday school class or accept other responsibilities which require regular attendance. Actually, they retrogress spiritually at the very time in life when they have a wonderful opportunity to grow into mature, beautiful Christians. They live for momentary earthly pleasures rather than abiding heavenly realities.

I am not implying that every Christian in his middle or later adult years should be present in his church 52 Sundays a year. Even pastors and Christian education directors get away for vacations. When people who are no longer confined by work or family responsibilities want to utilize their freedom by taking some weekends to visit friends and relatives, we have no right to criticize them. But in our plans, we should give priority to God and the local church. If we are in earnest about doing His will, we will find ways to enjoy some free time and still serve the Lord effectively.

Many churches today have organized their members into caring groups which provide the healthy with opportunities to serve those who have needs. These units are usually made up of people from each age bracket. The members meet from time to time, share their concerns, relate their experiences, and consider ways they can minister to the needs of the ill, the aged, the infirm, and the wayward assigned to them. Almost every able-bodied Christian, whether middle-aged or senior citizen, can be involved in this work. And when they are, they will not feel "over the hill" or useless.

KEEP LEARNING

Last, but by no means least, we should keep learning. We should never decide that we can no longer acquire new knowledge just because we have entered our middle or later years. Once a person takes this attitude, he is likely to retreat from active involvement in life and begin to feel unneeded. It is also quite likely that he will start repeating stories about the past and become a bore to his friends and relatives.

It's too bad that so many people have the mistaken idea that senility is a natural concomitant of the aging process. Actually, it is the general acceptance of this concept which has caused some senior citizens to have all the symptoms of senility. Assuming that they could no longer learn anything new, they started living in the past and gradually grew out of touch with the real world. Dr. William Glasser, a prominent advocate of "Reality Therapy," cites case histories of aged people brought back from what appeared to be hopeless senility. They were cured when they accepted assigned tasks and responsibilities which called on them to exercise creative thinking.

Dr. Carroll Freeman, a professor at New Orleans Baptist Theological Seminary, confirms these findings:

> The word "senility" is losing favor in the jargon of psychologists, psychiatrists, and general practitioners. One teacher of note has stated that senility is not a physical (organic) problem, but is emotional. It is a form of psychosis, or break with reality.
>
> Approximately 10 years ago psychologists from the University of Michigan came forth with data that indicated that the condition of three-

fourths of those committed to nursing homes could have been reversed. (Freeman, *The Senior Adult Years,* Broadman Press, 1979, p. 146.)

The Scriptures give us numerous examples of people who were mentally keen in old age. The patriarchs were lucid until the time of their death. Jacob was almost 150 when he called his sons to his bedside and declared to them a lengthy series of prophecies. Moses was clear-minded at the age of 120 when he climbed the mountain. The book of Luke introduces us to the aged Simeon and the 84-year-old widow Anna, both of whom recognized the baby Jesus as the Messiah of promise (Luke 2:25-38).

Closely related to the myth that older people normally become senile is the idea that they are severely handicapped in their learning ability. This erroneous concept may stem from the fact that some brain cells die every day, but the notion is perpetuated largely by older folks themselves. They quit trying to learn because they think they can't. Thus they fulfill what they assume to be true. Dr. Roger De Crow, a well-known scholar in the study of aging, makes the following pertinent comment:

> One of the strangest delusions in history is the still prevalent myth that older people cannot learn or that they typically suffer serious decline in mental abilities.

Common sense observation should dispel this notion, for hundreds of thousands of older adults are learning in the programs reported in our survey, and millions have learned every imaginable subject in adult education programs over the years and decades. (Roger DeCrow, *New Learning for Older Americans*, Washington: Adult Education Association Publishers, 1975, p. 12.)

He acknowledges that some older people may have a little disadvantage in learning exercises which require rapid detection of numbers or words. But he doesn't view this as a serious problem. A senior adult who doesn't learn well usually has some physical or psychological problem, not a mental handicap associated with aging itself.

Senior citizens can memorize, and do not need to be forgetful. Some older folks will disagree with this statement. When I made it to a Bible class of retirees, I encountered vehement protests. Most of them said they often forget where they put things—something they never did when they were younger. Others said they have given up all efforts to memorize because they simply can't do it. I am convinced, however, that they can remember and memorize as well as they ever did if they really want to.

One reason people forget is that it provides them with a ready excuse when they fail to do something they said they would. It isn't that they consciously say, "I'm going to make this promise and then forget it." The decision to "forget" occurs somewhere in the sub-conscious. Their conviction that they can't remember has programmed the mind to block out something they don't really care to recall.

Older folks also forget some things they remembered when they were younger because their interests have undergone a change. When they take off a watch, for example, they put it down without a second thought. They've been doing it for so many years that the act doesn't make much of an impression upon them. During their younger years they placed greater value upon the watch. They concentrated on the act of removing it and putting it away. If older folks would do this, they would remember just as well as they ever did.

This is also true with memorization. Young people give themselves more fully to what they are trying to memorize. Older people come to this task having their minds cluttered with worries, cares, and problems which they don't lay aside. Besides, memorization is hard work. It's far easier to say "I can't memorize any more" than to expend the energy required to do it.

Yes, if we keep studying, we will continue to grow in mental maturity, knowledge, and understanding. In that sense we are not "over the hill." We are still climbing. We live in a world designed and made by God. Though it is under the divine curse because of sin, it is still full of beauty and mystery. Therefore, we ought to take an interest in nature and the discoveries of science. We human beings are complex creatures made in the image of God but fallen because of sin. We ought to know as much about ourselves as we can. Current events affect the lives of all people everywhere and often include reminders of the Lord's second coming. Above all, the Bible teaches us everything we need to know about God, salvation, Christian conduct, and the glories that await us. Studying God's Word and memorizing passages from it will enable us to grow in the grace and knowledge of our Lord Jesus Christ.

Older people actually have some built-in advantages as they study. They have a wealth of knowledge and wisdom gained through experience which they can integrate with everything they learn. Senior adults have a unique ability to reflect upon themselves and to recall early life events with remarkable clarity. They can draw up memories from their subconscious, things they hadn't been aware of for years.

Therefore, a born-again believer who studies the Scriptures and reads good books can combine the knowledge he is now gaining with the memories from the past. This gives him a profound understanding not possible for the young. Then too, the older person who takes God's Word seriously may have opportunity to right some old wrongs, change some bad attitudes, and confess some sins which were never properly dealt with in the past.

The senior adult who studies and meditates upon spiritual realities will be gradually preparing himself for his appointment at the judgment seat of Christ. The combination of new insights with recollections from the past can help bring about a sense of peace and serenity in believers as they draw nearer the time of their departure. This attitude in turn enables them to find great enjoyment in elemental pleasures such as the sights, smells, and sounds of nature, the chatter and laughter of little children, and the quiet companionship of loved ones and friends. These blessings enable devoted Christians—even those who endure aches and pains—to find great happiness in the closing years of life.

In summary, no Christian need be depressed by that "over the hill" feeling which comes to so many people in their senior adult years. We can adjust our priorities so that we "seek . . . first the kingdom of God and His righteousness" (Matthew 6:33). We can strengthen our family ties. We can broaden our areas of concern. We can find ways to serve the Lord in our local church. And we can keep learning. We can make our last years the best of all.

5
THOSE LONELY HOURS

The death of a loved one always carries with it
a sense of sorrow and loss. This is true even
when the one taken is a Christian parent who
has reached a ripe old age or has been a
longtime invalid. It is especially painful to lose
a son or daughter. We have always thought in
terms of their surviving us, not vice versa. But
the passing of a marital partner produces a
poignant grief and oppressive loneliness
beyond that of any other loss. This is true
partly because the one-flesh relationship in
marriage is the closest of all earthly ties,
bringing into it a sharing of pain and disappointment, joy and aspiration. Besides, it
alters completely the lifestyle of the survivor.
Though we are deeply saddened by the death
of parents, brothers and sisters, and sons and

daughters, life goes on quite the same as it did before. But when a longstanding marriage ends, everything changes.

Since one member of almost every good marriage is going to go through the sorrow, grief, and shock of losing a mate, we ought to discuss this issue openly and honestly. We must confront it head-on. Therefore, in this chapter I offer five practical suggestions which I believe will prepare couples for this traumatic event and help the survivor when it happens. We Christians can take steps that will enable us to face the prospect of the death of a spouse with calmness and to handle it with grace when it happens.

EMOTIONAL PREPARATION

First, middle-aged men and women must willingly and openly acknowledge that one day—either soon or in the not-too-distant future—their earthly marital relationship will be severed by death. Granted, people who love one another don't find this a pleasant matter to contemplate. But we can be realistic without becoming morbid when we know the Lord. After all, we believe God's Word. And, if we walk with the Lord in daily fellowship, we possess a Spirit-imparted assurance that Heaven will be better than earth ever was. Deep within we have the confidence that all its relationships will be sweeter and richer than they are in this life. Though we realize that our marital relationship won't be resumed in its earthly form, we are confident that we will be special to one another for all eternity. Since we see the separation at death as only temporary, we can be honest in discussing this subject and making preparations for it.

I have often seen men and women taken by complete surprise at the death of a spouse. It appeared that they had never admitted the possibility of its happening to them. Some men normally well-organized are bewildered when a wife dies, and they admit that they made no plans for this contingency. Some women haven't the slightest idea about the state of their finances. Fortunately, most of them have relatives or friends who can help them. The lack of preparation in itself isn't a serious matter, but it reveals the fact that the bereaved are emotionally unprepared. This can be a real problem.

A couple of older people received a warning recently which caused them to face up to reality. Although they both had been ailing, they wouldn't discuss the possibility of death separating them. Then the husband suffered a heart attack which hospitalized him. His wife was an emotional wreck. The deacon in charge of a caring group at her church called on her immediately and learned that she was terrified at the thought of being alone at night. He made arrangements for some people to open their homes to her.

After 4 nights, however, someone suggested that these Christian friends were not really doing this woman a favor. They were not helping her prepare for the day when her husband will be taken. Therefore they gently suggested that she go back to her own house, and she consented. A grandson slept in the home to allay her fears but left for work early in the morning. This made it necessary for her to get her own breakfast and eat alone, which was good for her. She understood why it was being done and didn't object.

Her husband has returned home after a couple of weeks in the hospital, but it doesn't appear that he will live much longer. They are grateful beyond words for the privilege of being together again, but now they are beginning to face the future realistically. They have decided to sell their house, which requires a great deal of maintenance, and have made arrangements to purchase a small dwelling near some relatives. The husband is at peace, and the wife is making good progress in becoming emotionally adjusted to the prospect before her.

These folks had a warning, but everybody doesn't get one. How unwise to play the ostrich by ignoring reality! Life can end suddenly and without any warning. Admitting this, talking about it, and making plans for it—these are important steps in emotional preparation.

SPIRITUAL PREPARATION

Second, a husband and wife should make

specific spiritual preparation for this traumatic event. I am using the word "specific" because I know it is possible for a person to live a God-honoring Christian life without really preparing himself for this crushing blow. Sometimes people get well along in years without experiencing an overwhelming sorrow. Their parents lived to a ripe old age and died peacefully. Their brothers and sisters, and sons and daughters are all alive. They seem to assume that they will both reach an advanced age before death comes to either of them. Though they are genuine in their profession of faith in Christ and are ready to meet the Lord, they are not spiritually prepared for the shock of separation from one another through death. When one dies, the other is thrown into inconsolable grief.

We prepare ourselves spiritually for this traumatic event by our attitudes in the smaller trials and testings of life. We must learn to depend upon God even when the difficulty is relatively minor—even when we may be tempted to think we can handle it without special help. Christians blessed with good health, financial plenty, and a complete family circle may not learn to develop a humble trust in God. They've been able to handle the minor stresses and strains of life without much conscious dependence upon the Lord. Then, when struck by a major tragedy—like the loss of the marital partner—they can't cope. They lose every semblance of spiritual victory.

The apostle Peter, writing to Christians undergoing relatively mild persecution, emphasized the importance of placing all their confidence in God. He admonished them, "Humble yourselves, therefore, under the mighty hand of God, that He may exalt you in due time, casting all your care upon Him; for He careth for you" (1 Peter 5:6,7).

The exhortation "Humble yourselves . . . under the mighty hand of God" calls for us to place ourselves in the hands of the Lord just like a patient does when he entrusts himself to a surgeon. When we do this daily in the ordinary strains and stresses of life, we will develop a relationship with the Lord that will give us strength to meet the severest of all trials—the death of our marital partner.

The other part of Peter's admonition—"casting all your care upon Him"—enjoins us to commit the whole of our worries to God. We are to take each day's concerns to the Lord with the confident assurance that He will carry them for us. The peace God gives us day-by-day will also be ours when death severs earth's closest human bond.

Maybe you have noticed that some of the seemingly strongest and most self-reliant people fall apart when the mate dies, but that some of the more timid are amazingly composed at such a time. The reason for this is simple. Strong-minded and enterprising believers often fail to develop a pattern of humble submission and dependence. But the apprehensive and retiring individual has long since learned to do so.

It may be appropriate at this time to discuss another spiritual difficulty often associated with the death of a mate—deep feelings of guilt. The survivor begins to reflect upon the past and feel he didn't do all he could have done.

For example, an elderly man became bedridden, lost control of bodily functions, and needed a great deal of daily care. The wife wanted to keep him at home, and she did for a while. Her married children helped to bathe him, feed him, and keep him from developing bed sores. After a few months they jointly decided that they would do him a favor by placing him in a nursing home. He didn't like the idea and died within a month. Then they wondered if they had been too hasty. I told them that they had no reason to feel guilty. They did what they thought to be best! They had tried to keep him at home, but had found it to be impractical. When they meet this loved one in Heaven, they will have a happy reunion. They need not feel embarrassed at the thought of meeting him.

A man who wrote a book about his feelings at the time of his wife's death tells of the terrible guilt he felt after the funeral. He had found her dead on the floor when he returned home from an errand. He had been taking care of her for some time because she was recuperating from a stroke. She was still a partial invalid when a cerebral hemorrhage had taken her life. After he settled down to living alone, he started looking back upon their last months together. He began to think of all the ways in which he could have been nicer to her. He wished he had never lost his patience. He remembered times he could have encouraged her or spoken some special words of endearment but didn't. He began to weep uncontrollably. He even knelt by the bed and addressed her in the other world, asking her to forgive him. He also acknowledged his sin to God, shedding hot tears as he prayed.

The dreadful guilt feelings continued, however, until an old friend assured him that he had no reason to condemn himself so strongly. This wise Christian associate pointed out that he hadn't meant to be impatient. He showed him that during those months of caring for his invalid wife he had sometimes become irritable through sheer weariness. He assured him that his failure was due to his infirmity as an aged person more than evil, but that all elements of sin in his conduct had been placed under the blood of Christ. The friend further encouraged him by suggesting that his departed wife—if she remembered these unpleasant experiences at all—understood that they stemmed from his human weakness, not a lack of love. The guilt-ridden husband was greatly relieved by these assurances. Yet he carried some regrets with him to the end of his life.

We who are still together can take warning from this man's experience. Let's determine that with God's help we will be patient and cheerful with our loved one even when we are weary or inwardly distraught. The aches and pains and limitations that come with age sometimes make it difficult to be always sweet and loving with one another. But if we are conscious of this and seek the Lord's help, we can be patient, loving, and kind most of the time. Let's also pledge ourselves to do our best for our mate if he or she becomes ill or incapacitated. Take care of that marital partner at home as long as you can. But don't feel guilty if it becomes necessary to use the facilities of a hospital or nursing home.

If you have tried to be a good marriage partner, don't let second thoughts after your mate dies depress you. The devil wants to rob us of our Christian joy and victory. He likes to get us focusing upon the negatives of our past. We can all find much to regret when we look back and think of all the things we might have done differently. We must therefore reject these negative thoughts, seeing them as vain, worthless, and demoralizing. The best way to victory is to take the positive approach suggested by the apostle Paul. We read,

> Finally, brethren, whatever things are
> true, whatever things are honest,
> whatever things are just, whatever things
> are pure, whatever things are lovely,
> whatever things are of good report; if

there be any virtue, and if there be any praise, think on these things (Philippians 4:8).

If you have confessed your sins and failures, accept God's forgiveness, think positively, and go forward in the assurance that in Heaven you are going to have a delightful reunion with your former mate and all your loved ones who died in Christ.

In summary, we can prepare ourselves spiritually for the day when the one we love more than anyone else on earth will be taken from our side. We do so by humbly placing ourselves in God's hands at the beginning of each day, committing our anxieties to Him, confessing our sins, accepting His forgiveness, and depending upon the Holy Spirit to produce His fruit in us. With this life pattern we will lay a spiritual foundation upon which we will be able to stand firmly, come what may.

AVOID QUICK DECISIONS

My third suggestion to someone who has just lost a mate is: Don't make a quick decision about important matters. Our emotions can play tricks on us during the first few days after the death of a mate has occurred. Well-meaning relatives and friends, also operating under the control of their feelings, may make unwise suggestions. They may offer you favors sincerely but without thinking through all their implications. If you follow their advice or accept their generous invitations, you may be sorry later.

For example, a woman who had just lost her husband and was terribly apprehensive about living alone was invited to share the home of a close friend who had been a widow for several years. They agreed that the companionship would be good for both of them. All went well for a while, so the more recently bereaved woman sold her house and invested the money. But gradually the situation in the home started to change. A lot of tension began to develop between the women, and they concluded it would be best for them to live separately. However, the lady who had moved in with her friend was in a difficult position. She had been very happy in the house she had sold. She and her husband had lived there for almost 20 years. It was small, and the neighbors were good friends. But it now was gone and no house like it was available in that area. Besides, real estate had gone up, and the combination of this price rise plus double realtor fees would cause her to lose several thousand dollars. To make matters worse, some of the funds she had invested were not immediately available, and she would be penalized if she withdrew her time certificates. She stood to lose a lot of money, and she was not wealthy. How she wished she hadn't acted so impetuously!

A man with whom I am quite well

acquainted was about 80 years old when his wife was taken from him. The mobile home where they had lived until she went to the hospital was situated in a park, and they had many elderly friends. But now members of his family urged him to sell it and live with them. He wasn't sure about taking this step. Yet his emotional state was such that he wanted to please his family more than himself, so he followed their suggestion. However, after a year or so, he decided that living in with his children and grandchildren wasn't the answer. He looked into purchasing another mobile home in the area where he and his wife had lived, but none was available. So he consented to enter a rest home. He has a lovely room, and now after about 5 years is beginning to appreciate the convenience of his living arrangements. But he told me that the time between his wife's passing and the present could have been far happier if he hadn't made such a quick decision under pressure from his family. They meant well, but they didn't give him good advice.

Don't let your loved ones and friends talk you into a major decision at the time your mate dies. We all tend to be led by our emotions rather than good common sense when we are overwhelmed by grief and sympathy. If you have made plans, stick by them for a time at least. If you haven't, postpone major decisions until you can think clearly and can discuss the Lord's leading.

BE AGREEABLE AND SOCIABLE

My fourth suggestion to a man or woman left after the death of the marital partner is: Accept graciously the small kindnesses offered by relatives and friends, and be sociable. Sometimes bereaved people want to be left alone. They are depressed and don't like the thought of being with people, not even with close relatives. As a result, they tend to decline invitations to meals and a variety of suitable social functions.

Of course, some privacy is essential for grieving people. In a time of sorrow we need periods of being alone so that we can sort out our thoughts and line up our feelings with our faith. But we also need human companionship. No Christian should draw a circle around himself and keep everybody outside of it.

Remember, the Scriptures often portray believers at their best in association with others of like faith. The men and women who accepted Christ on that memorable Pentecost described in Acts 2 banded together immediately. In Acts 2:42 we read that they "continued steadfastly in the apostles' doctrine and fellowship, and in breaking of bread, and in prayers."

Furthermore, the Bible declares sociability to be a characteristic of the Spirit-filled believer. Paul wrote,

> And be not drunk with wine, in which is excess, but be filled with the Spirit,

> Speaking to yourselves in psalms
> and hymns and spiritual songs, singing
> and making melody in your heart to the
> Lord (Ephesians 5:18,19).

Christians who are morose and reject fellowship with others after the death of a mate contradict the very truth they profess to believe. If death really "is gain" and absence from the body really means being "with Christ," as Paul declares in Philippians 1 and in 2 Corinthians 5, a bereaved child of God should be rejoicing even in sorrow. What can be more wonderful than being in company with fellow believers and joining them in prayers and praises? It follows, therefore, that we ought to accept the attention and fellowship of Christian loved ones and friends, and that we should love to be with the family of God.

Sometimes people who seclude themselves after the death of a mate, refusing all invitations and attending very few church services, have every intention of coming out of their shell eventually. But they are in danger of developing a state of mind which causes them to shrink from close social contacts. They injure their capacity to be friendly and warm. Besides, their relatives and friends may assume that they don't want to be bothered with visits or invitations. They quit trying. Therefore, you should accept invitations and respond favorably to tokens of friendship even when you may prefer being alone. Usually you'll be glad you did.

If you have become somewhat of a recluse, you can do something about it. Start attending church faithfully, participate in all the activities you can, and invite a few people to be your guests in your home. If you can afford it, you may want to ask a couple of friends to go to a restaurant with you. Once people see that you really desire fellowship, they will begin reaching out to you. Remember, we all need one another's friendship and love.

THINK POSITIVELY

Finally, the bereaved husband or wife must think positively. No, I am not advocating the exercise of a superficial "everything's going to be fine" kind of wishful thinking. A child of God doesn't need to project a dream world. We believe the holy Scriptures, and we have good grounds for our conviction that they are true. We are confident that God loves us and that He has a purpose for everything He permits in our lives. We are assured that He will one day glorify all who have placed their trust in Jesus Christ. Let's meditate upon these truths until they permeate all our thinking.

If you have been left alone through the death of your mate, remember with gratitude to God the good things of the past. Banish unpleasant memories! Thank the Lord again for His salvation. Remind yourself that all your sins and failures are under the blood. Memorize Bible passages like Romans 8:28. You will gain the confidence that the most distressing of all your experiences have been woven into the pattern of your life for your eventual welfare. Think back gratefully!

You should also reflect upon the needs of people around you and ask the Lord to show you what He wants you to do in the here and now. You have been left on earth for a purpose. As mentioned earlier, believers always reap joy and satisfaction from giving of themselves for others. Our prayers, our kind words, our encouraging smiles, and our loving deeds will pay rich dividends both here and hereafter.

Then too, let's look forward with hope and expectation. We are on our way to Heaven. Jesus is there. Our loved ones who died believing on Him are there. So are the saints of all the ages. One day we're going to see Jesus. We're going to be welcomed by loved ones and friends who've gone ahead of us. We're going to join that great company portrayed in Hebrews 11. We may have a few hard places along the way, but we're on the right road. Heaven will be our eternal Home! What a glorious prospect! Let's keep it in view!

In conclusion, we need not live in dread of the day our mate will be taken from our side. God's grace will give us strength if and when we are left alone. Therefore, let's prepare ourselves emotionally by discussing the matter openly and honestly. Let's get ready spiritually by walking in humble dependence, careful obedience, and beautiful submission to the Lord. Let's avoid hasty decisions when we are bereft of our loved one, accept the kind offers of friends and relatives, and think positively about the past, present, and future. Yes, we can experience peace and joy during those lonely hours after a lifelong mate is taken from us.

6
THOSE LEISURE YEARS

One day recently I saw Les, a man who once served as a deacon in a church I pastored. I knew he was now retired, and I asked him how he liked it. His reply was, "Great! In fact, I like it so well I would have enjoyed making a career out of it." I watched him walk briskly to his car, and could tell that he was a happy retiree. I also knew why. His days are just as full as they ever were. He is active in his church, serves with the Gideons, and is finding numerous ways to work for the Lord. He's doing things now for which he never had enough time when he was working.

It would be wonderful if everybody enjoyed retirement like this man does. Sad to say, many folks don't. They become unhappy, frustrated, and bored soon after they leave their jobs. Some singles become terribly lonely. Couples who had a good marriage may start having marital problems.

Let me tell you about Harry. (That's not his real name, but represents a person I know.) He had worked in the same factory for 42 years. His job required some skill, but once learned, it tended to be rather monotonous. Still, he didn't really mind his task and didn't dread going to work. He actually looked forward to each day because he had a warm regard for some of the people at the shop. But when he reached the age of 60, he began thinking about retirement. He thought it would be great to get away from punching that timeclock every morning. He considered accepting Social Security when he was 62, but he and his wife decided it would be wise to work another 3 years.

All went well until he celebrated his 64th birthday. During that last year he counted the months, weeks, and days. He could hardly wait. When the magic moment finally arrived, his associates had a farewell party for him. He knew it wasn't a big deal, but he enjoyed it. They gave him a small gift, congratulated him, and said their goodbys. They made him feel like he was the most fortunate of all men. "Harry, you lucky dog, now you can sleep in every morning." "What a life you're going to have! Nothing to do but relax and fish." "I hope you'll think of us poor slaves while you're having your fun."

Harry went home full of joy and anticipation. His wife shared his excitement. They looked forward to enjoying some years of leisure. But today, a little more than 12 months later, Harry is sitting around like a man waiting to die. He is bored. His wife isn't very happy either. The two of them are bickering a lot more than they used to.

The problem is that Harry and his wife hadn't planned for their retirement. They don't know what to do with their time. They can't afford much traveling and they get tired of fishing. Harry has decided that if he can find a good part-time job he will accept it.

The number of people who share the quandary of this couple is increasing every year. More than 20 million in the United States alone are in the "over 65" age bracket. Government projections are 33 million by the year 2000. Just one-third of that number becoming depressed, bored, and disgruntled like Harry and his wife will add up to a lot of misery.

Anyone who knows a few unhappy retirees and does some thinking about the statistics will agree that middle-aged people should plan carefully for their retirement. Therefore, in this chapter I'm going to sound like a preacher by presenting two exhortations to those getting ready for their leisure years. First, plan for inevitable adjustments. Second, utilize your new situation to enrich your life and to prepare for eternity. People who have already entered the rest phase of life can't turn the calendar back, but I believe they will be able to transform their remaining years if they will apply the principles set forth in this chapter.

PLAN FOR ADJUSTMENTS

Everyone who is nearing retirement should begin to think seriously about the adjustments which will be demanded by this new way of life. Leaving active employment greatly alters a person's routine. Some of the changes won't come easily. The daily pattern of many years has been deeply etched upon the inner self. Retirees will therefore experience some trauma as they start to modify their activities. The day-by-day pattern will be much different. Home life will undergo drastic readjustments. Recreation won't be anything like it used to be. Income may be smaller. If a person retires without having considered these vast deviations from his former lifestyle, he is likely to become terribly frustrated and unhappy.

A New Routine

The first major rearrangement will be the daily schedule. A person who has been accustomed to getting up at 6 o'clock five days a week with 2 added hours on Saturday and Sunday may think it's going to be great to sleep in until 9 o'clock every morning. But he probably won't be able to do so. After a few days he'll start getting up almost as early as he did when he was working. He's also likely to have mixed feelings about not going to work. He'll be glad he isn't under the obligation to punch the timeclock every morning. He'll be happy that he won't have to put up with the irritations of his job. But he will likely also feel somewhat empty, useless, and unfulfilled.

If you are under 65, in reasonably good health, enjoying your work, and under no pressure to quit, you may be wise to consider seriously whether or not you want to stay on a few more years. It is also possible that you should think in terms of a part-time job. Or you may want to offer your services as a volunteer in serving the Lord or some community project. In any situation, be sure to think ahead. Even if you have an unusual love for reading and study, you had better prepare for some other activities. You're not going to be happy doing almost nothing.

Home Life

Another area of major adjustment relates to the home. This is true for people who are living alone as well as for couples. A full-time job usually pulls a person out of the house for at least 50 hours a week. After retirement many of these hours are spent at home. This can be the cause of serious problems both for singles and marrieds.

A woman who lives alone said that while she was employed she looked forward to doing a thorough job of cleaning and painting all the rooms in her house. At retirement she got right at it, did it with enthusiasm, and completed her project quickly. She expected to derive great pleasure from her leisure time, but after a few days of resting she became bored and lonely. She almost wished she could go back to work. She had made the mistake of making no plans for her leisure hours and as a result her home became a place of boredom and depression instead of pleasure and joy.

Retired couples often discover that being together all the time is too much of what they thought would be a good thing. Statistics indicate that among non-Christians the early retirement years are marked by a high divorce rate. Many people who had a fairly good marriage through the years of employment and child-rearing find it difficult to cope with retirement. I don't think a large percentage of Christians in their leisure years head for the divorce courts, but I'm afraid that many of them lose the closeness they had in the past. They start to argue more and enjoy one another less.

A fine believer with whom I am well acquainted realized that he and his wife wouldn't be happy sitting in the house just looking at one another. They don't care about traveling, and neither of them likes golf, tennis, or bowling. He made sure, therefore, that he had some land and was prepared to raise some animals when he retired. He soon discovered that this was a very wise move. One morning as he sat at a desk doing some paper work, he noticed that his wife was irritable. She frankly told him she wanted him out of the house right after breakfast and devotions. From long habit she had made the bed, washed the dishes, and tidied up the house before noon. This pattern had become deeply ingrained. She instinctively wanted to be alone during the morning hours. He recognized this and cooperated. He kids her about her hang-up and she responds good-naturedly. They have no serious problem because they had planned for the adjustments that would come when he quit his job.

Colena M. Anderson tells how a couple named Bill and Martha adjusted to their new togetherness. He had retired in early June. At first he and his wife had found their new freedom to be exhilarating. They took several weekend trips out of state. They visited friends they hadn't seen for years. They occasionally spent a day at a nearby park which bordered on a beach. Bill enjoyed his garden. He grew the best flowers on the block and shared vegetables with neighbors. But one day his wife made a remark which made him realize that his being out of the house meant more to her than the vegetables he grew. But it wasn't until a rainy Saturday in September that he found out how much she wanted him outside for part of each day. He happened to be in the family room watching a re-run of a football game when she came in with the vacuum cleaner. He obligingly moved three times to get out of her way. Suddenly she turned off the cleaner and said, "Bill, I wish you'd leave me alone here to finish this room. Go out to the garden, or take a walk. Go see how Jeff is getting along" (*Don't Put On Your Slippers Yet*, Zondervan, 1971, p. 20).

Her reference to Jeff, the talking parrot in the print shop, told Bill that she would rather have him at work than at home. He was hurt, but did not argue. He put on his raincoat and walked to his former place of employment. He greeted the Saturday crew, people with whom he had worked. He then approached his boss and asked about the possibility of obtaining a part-time position. The response was a reluctant no. The shop didn't have an opening at this time.

After staying in the print shop for a while, Bill slowly made his way back home. As he reflected, he began to understand why Martha felt the way she did. After all, her work continued to be almost exactly like it was before he had retired. His being in the house so much of the time made it harder for her to maintain her unwritten but deeply ingrained schedule. He decided to go into the custom printing business as a part-time venture. He can take pride in this work because it is something he can do well. Therefore, it is more satisfying than gardening. Best of all, it keeps him from getting on his wife's nerves.

In concluding this section, I would like once again to remind single people that it is tremendously important for them to make plans for retirement. If you don't, you may find yourself unable to cope well with the long hours of being alone. You may be tempted to make an effort to escape the real world by becoming engrossed with television, staying up until the wee hours of the morning and sleeping till noon. All the while you will experience disappointment because your retirement isn't anything like you had expected it to be. And you will feel guilty about wasting your precious time. My advice, therefore, is to have a carefully structured plan which will get you out of your house and into the stream of life.

If you are a middle-aged married person, discuss with your mate the anticipated changes in your home life. Make a joint decision about the things the two of you can enjoy together. Then talk about your individual needs which relate to the home. It may be wise for the husband to build himself a small workshop in the basement or to convert a spare room into a study. This will give the wife times during the day when she can be alone. If two people love one another and aim at being unselfish, they will be willing and able to make the adjustments necessary for a happy home after retirement. But these new arrangements can best be implemented when they have been anticipated.

Recreation

Another adaptation for retirees must be made in their recreation. Fishing may be fun when you do it during your time off from work, but it can become a drag when it is the only thing you can do. This is true of almost any pastime, including sports like golfing and bowling. In fact, the word "recreation" carries the thought of a renewal of the body and spirit after either mental or physical toil. The weariness that comes from playing ball, jogging, or working in the garden is a good feeling for someone who spends his days at a desk. The thinking involved in playing chess, reading, or learning a new language may be refreshing for someone who is an administrator or works with his hands. But when a person retires and these activities become his main occupation, he will find that they lose their recreational nature.

A retiree, therefore, should not think in terms of spending practically all of his waking hours on a lake or at the golf course. He won't find these times as enjoyable as he once did. He may also start feeling guilty when he realizes that he is seeking pleasure above everything else. A healthy person planning retirement must build at least a few worthwhile functions into his schedule. This will help him feel good about himself, allow his pastimes to be truly recreative, and help him enjoy his leisure years.

Income

A third adjustment for many retirees involves less income. I said "many retirees" because some have enough returns from investments, pensions, and Social Security to live as lavishly as they please. Others have had such a conservative lifestyle that their reduced earnings will only mean that they will have a smaller amount to put into savings. But a lower standard of living will be mandatory for folks who have lived in a large home, have grown accustomed to quite a bit of traveling, or have indulged in a variety of expensive recreational activities.

Every prospective retiree should confront his or her new economic status with honesty and realism. It may be wise to sell the large home and buy one suitable for one or two persons. Less expensive forms of recreation may be necessary. The adjustments in lifestyle should be anticipated and accepted before retirement rather than reluctantly made afterward.

UTILIZE YOUR NEW SITUATION

Since we are left here on earth to glorify God and prepare ourselves for Heaven, we should utilize our retirement years to promote our own spiritual development and to serve Him. If we who are Christians plan our leisure only in terms of personal enjoyment, we won't promote our true happiness. Moreover, we'll close out our earthly pilgrimage as spiritual failures.

Since we've already discussed the importance of being good church members and remaining useful in the Lord's work, we need not go over that ground again. But we can profitably consider the unique opportunity of retirees to nurture an effective devotional life, to use their skills in witnessing, and to touch the lives of people with kind and considerate acts.

Devotional Life

Every retired believer should place a high priority on his or her own individual spiritual growth. When we are actively engaged in making a living, we sometimes let ourselves get too busy. We think we cannot take an hour a day for Scripture reading, good books, and prayer. We may also have problems concentrating when we do get around to studying and praying. Our concerns and cares intrude. When we retire, however, we no longer live under these occupational pressures and schedule demands. It becomes much easier to maintain a rich devotional life.

Older people, especially those who have time on their hands, must remember that temptation knows no age barrier. Our added years by themselves do not make us immune to bad thoughts and solicitations to evil. In fact, our failings and our strengths tend

105

to crystallize when we reach our senior adult years.

For example, a woman who has had a lifelong tendency to nag will drive her husband crazy if she doesn't recognize this fault and get the Lord's help to overcome it. A man who has often allowed his mind to dwell on lustful thoughts is likely to become the proverbial "dirty old man" when he reaches his sixties, unless he takes this sinful proclivity to the Lord. We need a close walk with Him or our worst characteristics will take charge of us.

Then too, retirement can open the door for the devil to tempt God's children. It was when David remained at home doing nothing while his soldiers went to battle that he lusted after Bath-sheba, committed adultery with her, and secured the death of her husband. How important to keep in touch with the Lord during our leisure years!

Finally, we must build and maintain a solid devotional life as we prepare for retirement because we have a calling to fulfill. God has predestined us to be like Christ, and it won't be long before our time on earth will be ended and we shall stand in His presence.

Witnessing

The retirement years also give us a golden opportunity to witness effectively through the use of our skills. When we were raising our children and working for a living we could witness verbally and be helpful, but we always operated under the limitations of a busy schedule. After retirement we have more time.

A woman who is an excellent cook can provide a meal for a neighboring family where the wife and mother is ill or in the hospital. If she bakes a super cherry pie, she may want to take one along when she greets folks who have just moved into the community. The man who is able to perform small plumbing and carpenter jobs can use these skills to help people in the name of the Lord Jesus.

A retired minister in a small community checks the obituary columns in the local newspaper and sends a personal letter of sympathy to the bereaved family. After giving them some general words of comfort, He presents the gospel and offers free counsel. His name, address, and telephone number are on the stationery. He says this ministry is very fruitful.

Retirement offers us a marvelous chance to use our areas of competence as a means of witnessing for Christ.

Small Kindnesses

Another way we can utilize our retirement to serve the Lord is through simple kindnesses which require no special skill. Many people will tell you that a phone call or an appropriate card can brighten an entire day.

A lady in her eighties makes it a point to

know which young people in her church and her immediate neighborhood are graduating from high school and sends them a congratulatory card with a brief note. She also sends appropriate greetings to shut-ins, the hospitalized, and the grieving. Many people, both young and old, have expressed their appreciation to her.

Another elderly woman, whose husband is an invalid and in a nursing home, telephones people she knows to be just as lonely as she is. She is positive and uplifting in her conversation. Two aged widows have told me that when they hear the phone ringing in the late evening hours they find themselves saying, "That's probably Iris." They are disappointed if they don't hear from her for several days.

Yes, retirees can touch the lives of people around them. It will cost them a little bit of money and quite a bit of time. But the rewards are great. Only eternity will reveal how much is accomplished through these small acts of kindness.

In conclusion, our leisure stage of life can be happy and useful if we plan for the adjustments it will demand and utllize its new opportunities to glorify God. Freed from the pressure of making a living or raising a family, we can use much of our time for personal growth and spiritual impact. Let's avoid the common failings of older people, talking about our aches and pains, living in the past, or speaking as if we possess all wisdom. By walking in daily fellowship with the Lord we can radiate the spirit of Christ. Yes, even from a wheelchair or a bed of pain, we can be positive in our influence.

The psalmist portrayed the blessedness and fruitfulness of the aged who know the Lord when he wrote,

> The righteous will flourish like a palm tree, they will grow like a cedar of Lebanon; planted in the house of the Lord, they will flourish in the courts of our God. They will still bear fruit in old age, they will stay fresh and green, proclaiming, "The Lord is upright; He is my Rock, and there is no wickedness in Him" (Psalm 92:12-15 NIV).

The fact that our retirement years represent the close of life's earthly journey should not trouble us if we know the Lord. We need fear neither death itself nor the judgment which will follow. Our Savior paid the complete price for all our sin by His death on the cross, and broke death's power by His glorious resurrection. That's why the apostle Paul personified death after he had explained the doctrine of the resurrection, hurled two questions at it, provided the answer, and issued this ringing challenge:

> "Where, O death, is your victory?
> Where, O death, is your sting?"

The sting of death is sin, and the power

of sin is the law. But thanks be to God! He gives us the victory through our Lord Jesus Christ.

Therefore, my dear brothers, stand firm. Let nothing move you. Always give yourselves fully to the work of the Lord, because you know that your labor in the Lord is not in vain (1 Corinthians 15:55-58 NIV).

When we reach our retirement years, the shadows of life will have lengthened to the east, reminding us that our day is almost done. But we who know the Lord have the joyous assurance that a bright new morning will dawn for us on the shores of Heaven. There we will see our Savior, hear His words of approval, and be rewarded for all our labors on this side. What a glorious prospect! What an incentive to loving devotion and willing service right down to the end of our earthly pilgrimage!